ASIAN
COUNTRIES
TODAY

VIETNAM

ASIAN
COUNTRIES
TODAY

CHINA
INDONESIA
JAPAN
MALAYSIA
PHILIPPINES
SINGAPORE
SOUTH KOREA
THAILAND
VIETNAM

VIETNAM

JENNIFER BROWN

MASON CREST
PHILADELPHIA
MIAMI

MASON CREST

450 Parkway Drive, Suite D, Broomall, Pennsylvania 19008
(866) MCP-BOOK (toll-free) • www.masoncrest.com

Printed in the United States of America

First printing
9 8 7 6 5 4 3 2 1

ISBN (hardback) 978-1-4222-4272-8
ISBN (series) 978-1-4222-4263-6
ISBN (ebook) 978-1-4222-7558-0

Cataloging-in-Publication Data on file with the Library of Congress

Developed and Produced by National Highlights Inc.
Editor: Susan Uttendorfsky
Interior and cover design: Jana Rade
Production: Michelle Luke

NATIONAL
HIGHLIGHTS

CONTENTS

KEY ICONS TO LOOK FOR:

WORDS TO UNDERSTAND: These words with their easy-to-understand definitions will increase the reader's understanding of the text while building vocabulary skills.

SIDEBARS: This boxed material within the main text allows readers to build knowledge, gain insights, explore possibilities, and broaden their perspectives by weaving together additional information to provide realistic and holistic perspectives.

EDUCATIONAL VIDEOS: Readers can view videos by scanning our QR codes, providing them with additional educational content to supplement the text. Examples include news coverage, moments in history, speeches, iconic sports moments, and much more!

TEXT-DEPENDENT QUESTIONS: These questions send the reader back to the text for more careful attention to the evidence presented there.

RESEARCH PROJECTS: Readers are pointed toward areas of further inquiry connected to each chapter. Suggestions are provided for projects that encourage deeper research and analysis.

SERIES GLOSSARY OF KEY TERMS: This back-of-the-book glossary contains terminology used throughout this series. Words found here increase the reader's ability to read and comprehend higher-level books and articles in this field.

China

Myanmar

Laos

Thailand

Vietnam

Cambodia

Sri Lanka

Brunei

Malaysia

°Singapore

Inc

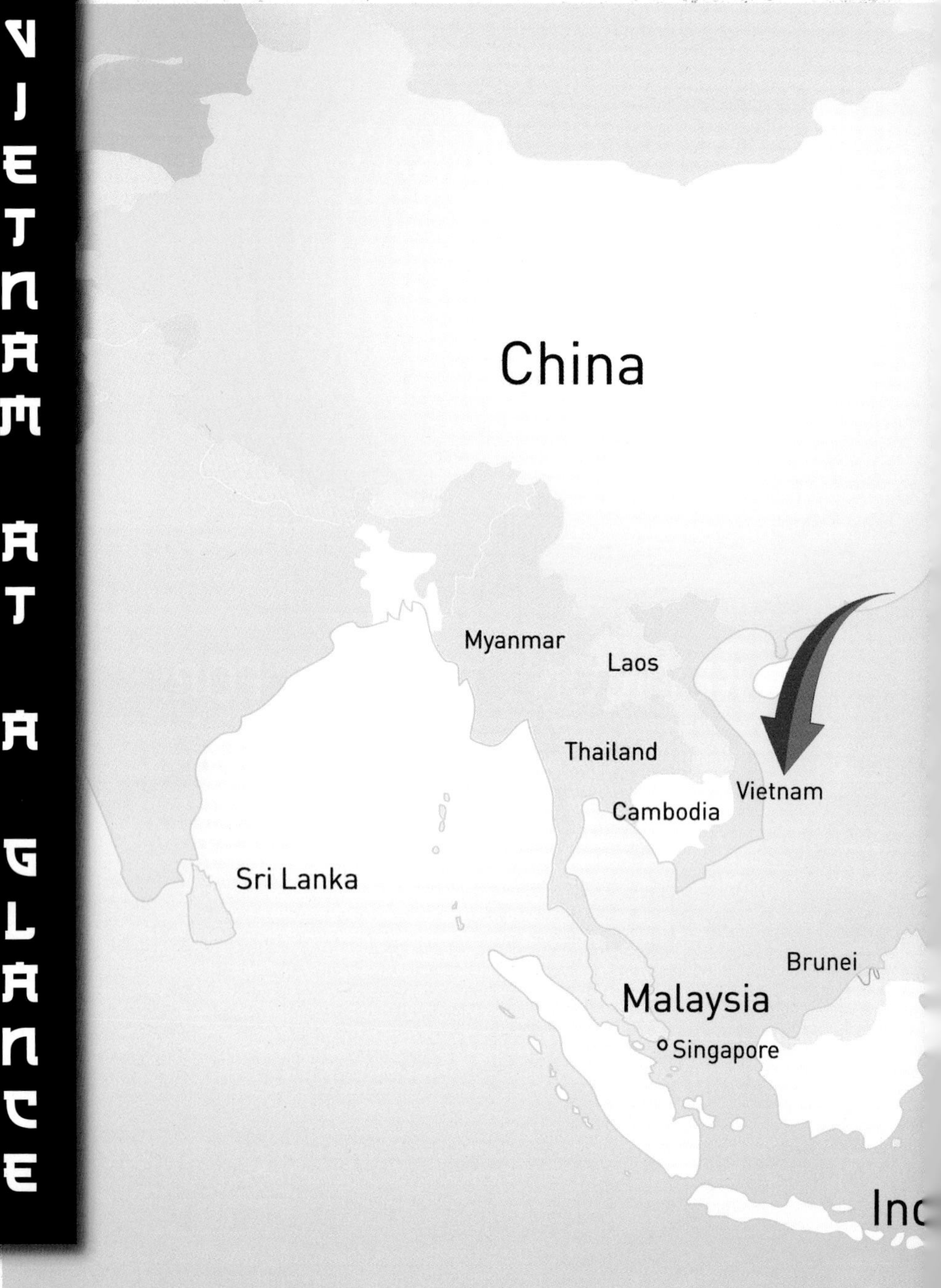

North Korea

South Korea

Japan

ilippines

The Geography of Vietnam

Location:
Southeastern Asia, and borders the Gulf of Thailand, the Gulf of Tonkin, and the South China Sea, along with Cambodia, Laos, and China

Area: Slightly larger than New Mexico
total: 331,210 square miles (533,030 sq. km)
land: 310,070 square miles (499,009 sq. km)
water: 21,140 square miles (34,021 sq. km)

Borders: Laos, China, Cambodia

Climate: Tropical in the south, while the north is monsoonal with a rainy, hot season that lasts from the months of May to September, as well as a dry, warm season that lasts from October to March

Terrain: Low and flat delta located in the north and south; central highlands; and in the north and northwest, a mountainous and hilly area

Elevation Extremes:
lowest point: South China Sea at exactly sea level

highest point: Fan Si Pan 10,314 feet (3,144 m) above sea level

Natural Hazards:
Typhoons and flooding

The flag of Vietnam is a red background with a single gold star. It was originally designed in 1940 during a time when there was an uprising against the French rule in the southern part of Vietnam. The red color symbolizes the goals held by the social revolution that was behind the national uprising in Vietnam. The flag was officially adopted by the country on September 5, 1945.

The People of Vietnam

Population: 97,040,334

Ethnic Groups: Kinh (Viet), Tay, Muong, Khmer, Nung, Hoa, other

Age Structure:
0–14 years: 23.27% (22,581,036)
15–24 years: 15.81% (15,338,997)
25–54 years: 45.67% (44,318,693)
55–64 years: 8.9% (8,634,799)
65 years and over: 6.35% (6,166,809)

Population Growth Rate:
0.9%

Death Rate:
5.9 deaths/1,000 pop.

Migration Rate:
-0.3 migrant(s)/1,000 pop.

Infant Mortality Rate:
16.7 deaths/1,000 live births

Life Expectancy at Birth:
total population: 73.9 years
male: 71.4 years
female: 76.7 years

Total Fertility Rate:
1.79 children born/woman

Religions:
Buddhist, Catholic, Hoa Hao, Cao Dai, Protestant, Muslim

Languages:
Vietnamese, English, French, Chinese, and Khmer, mountain area languages (Mon-Khmer and Malayo-Polynesian)

Literacy Rate:
94.5%

Source: www.cia.gov 2018

The impressive limestone rock formations at Ha Long Bay in north Vietnam.

Communist: a person or country who believes or supports the principles of communism

indigenous: produced, growing, living, or occurring naturally in a particular region or environment

karst: an irregular geological ecosystem with porous limestone containing sinkholes, underground streams, and caverns

monsoon: a wind system, accompanied by heavy rains, that influences large regions and reverses direction seasonally

CHAPTER 1

VIETNAM'S GEOGRAPHY & LANDSCAPE

O nce a one-party **Communist** state, Vietnam currently has one of the fastest growing economies in Southeast Asia, with aspirations to become a developed nation by the year 2020. The lush mountains, golden sand beaches, and bustling cities attract visitors year after year, and while there is much modernization in Ho Chi Minh City (formerly Saigon), there are still countless, time-honored traditions that remain intact among the local residents.

The country of Vietnam is made up of mountains covered in dense forests, rolling green hills, and tropical lowlands. Approximately 20 percent of the country is considered low-level land.

One of the most agriculturally important areas is the Red River Delta, with hills that rise gently into the higher mountains to the northwest, while the Annam Highlands cover much of the bigger, central landscape. There's a fertile, yet narrow, coastal lowland that extends from the south of the Red River Delta, reaching the Mekong Delta. The geography of Vietnam is suited for the agricultural industry that the country thrives on and provides rich, fertile lands for growing food and other resources.

Geography

Vietnam is a long and narrow country made up of various geographical regions. A coastal plain runs along the east side of the country. However, most of the country is made up of densely forested mountains. Approximately 20 percent of the entire country is covered by low-level land where the majority of its citizens live.

A narrow yet fertile coastal lowland extends south from the Red River Delta all the way to the Mekong Delta. This low-lying, level plain was once covered by hundreds of different canals and small rivers. The far southern part of the country is swathed in mangrove swamps and thick jungles.

The most significant rivers in Vietnam include the Mekong and the Red River, also known as Song Hong. Each has several tributaries, and the Mekong is considered one of the great rivers in the entire world. The highest point in Vietnam is Fan Si Pan, with the lowest point being the South China Sea.

The source of the water that flows into the Red River Delta comes from the hills above it that rise gently into the higher mountains of the northwest region. The Annam Highlands cover quite a bit of the central landscape, and in the southern regions, coastal lowlands merge with the Mekong River Delta.

The Climate

Vietnam's climate is divided into temperate and tropical zones. It is known for the strong **monsoon** influences and the country receives a good amount of sun, a high level of rainfall, and high levels of humidity, which can make the region feel somewhat uncomfortable. The areas further north and close to the mountains have a temperature that's somewhat cooler, with a more temperate climate.

Annually, the average temperature of Vietnam ranges from 71° Fahrenheit (22° Celsius) to 80° Fahrenheit (27° Celsius) throughout the year. There are usually no great differences in the temperature in Vietnam's southern regions, but the northern areas are often quite cold during the winter months. There are four distinct seasons that are mostly experienced in the northern part of the country.

In the southern areas, there are only two distinguishable seasons. Between the months of November and April, Vietnam experiences a cold season, while the hot season occurs between the months of May and October.

Lightweight, cotton clothing is a good idea at any time during the year, with the addition of a raincoat and umbrella for sudden rainstorms during the summer when temperatures and humidity are high. Sweaters and warmer clothing options are needed during the winter when visiting the northern regions.

According to the Koppel-Geiger Climate Classification, southern Vietnam has an Awe climate, which means it is tropical and hot with virtually all months being over 64.4° Fahrenheit (18° Celsius), with a dry period in the winter months. The northern regions of Vietnam are classified as a Cwa climate, with a temperate

Flooding following a monsoon in the ancient town of Hoi An in Quang Nam Province.

climate and the warmest months having a temperature of 71.6° Fahrenheit (22° Celsius) and the coldest months ranging between 64.4° and 26.6° Fahrenheit (18° Celsius and -3° Celsius), with a dryer period during the winter months.

Waterways

Vietnam has exactly 25,476 miles (41,000 km) of natural waterways, with 4,970 miles (8,000 km) of these used commercially. Of all these, the Inland Waterways Administration of Vietnam is responsible for managing approximately 3,728 miles (6,000 km) of these, in addition to the primary river ports. Local governments manage the balance of the other commercial waterways.

Barges and river boats have expanded rapidly, with 63,600 units present in 1999 with a capacity of 1.7 million dead weight tons, along with 197,000 passenger seats.

Learn about the unique geography of Vietnam in this video.

Nga Nam is a floating market in Soc Trang that is situated along the Mekong Delta.

The country's coastline spans 3,260 miles (5,246 km) and borders the South China Sea, Gulf of Tonkin, and Thailand. Vietnam is a coastal country and has several major seaports, which include Nha Trang, Vung Tau, Qui Nho'n, Hong Gai, Ho Chi Minh City, Hai Phong, Da Nang, and Cam Ranh. The network of rivers in Vietnam plays a significant role in rural transportation, with more than 11,000 miles (17,702 km) total of navigable waterways for water taxis, barges, and ferries.

The majority of the population of Vietnam lives near or along the Mekong Delta, as well as the Red River Delta. In fact, Hanoi and Ho Chi Minh City are situated close to the Red River and Mekong deltas.

Hội An is on the central coast of Vietnam and best known for its Ancient Town, which is perfectly preserved and cut through by canals. Formerly a major port city, Hội An's diverse history is clearly depicted in the amazing architecture, mixing an array of styles and eras from wooden temples and shop houses inspired from China to colonial buildings inspired by the French. However, there's still quite a bit of traditional culture seen here, thanks to the tube houses, the Japanese-style covered bridges, and beautiful pagodas.

The Hoai River is a tributary of the Thu Bon River that runs through Hội An. It is considered to be one of the most beautiful rivers in the entire world. This waterway is not only important to the area but is also a huge tourist attraction. Home to countless commercial boats as well as tours, the river is always buzzing with activity.

Flora and Fauna

Vietnam is considered to be one of the most biologically diverse countries in the entire world. It is home to a large array of fascinating and distinctive animals and plants.

Vietnam is located where the tropical ecosystems of Southeast Asia meet mainland Asia's temperate ecosystems, and it stretches more than 1,025 miles (1,650 km) from the north

Cat Ba langurs

The Cat Ba langur is one of several different langur species (a type of monkey) that are found in the limestone areas of Vietnam, which means that their natural habitat is found primarily in karsts. These animals sleep in caves, which protects them from the often unfavorable weather conditions. A single group of langurs may inhabit several (up to twelve) caves as their resting sites. In most cases, they only stay in the same cave for one or two nights before moving to another resting and feeding area.

Female and male langurs have virtually identical coloration, and the only difference is a white pubic patch on the females. The infants are a flamboyant orange, and they only start to develop the adult coloration—overall blackish, but the crown, cheeks, and neck are white—when they turn four months of age.

to the south. With an environment that ranges from cooler mountain ecosystems found in the northern Himalayan foothills to striking **karst** landscapes and tropical forests in the south, several unique species are found here.

There are currently more than 10,000 animal species and over 13,200 terrestrial plant species in Vietnam, with approximately 3,000 aquatic species found in the wetland locations. While the plant and animal life are vast, primates are the most striking of all of the natural treasures in Vietnam. Twenty-five **indigenous** different primate species live here, with eleven being critically endangered and five are only found in the country of Vietnam. Several others are only located in Southeast Asia. This makes Vietnam one of the most important countries in the world when it comes to the conservation of primates.

The vegetation in Vietnam is extremely diverse, which accurately reflects the country's varied climate, soils, topography, and human habitation. Forests in

These juvenile Cat Ba langurs are tinged with yellow. The older ones have white heads.

Vietnam are classified into two main categories: evergreen forests, which include conifers, and deciduous forests. Currently, there are over 1,500 different woody plants in Vietnam that range from hardwoods, which are commercially important, to woody vines and various herbaceous plants. Open and dense forests, savannas, bamboo, and brushland cover almost 50 percent of the country's total area.

In the majority of Vietnam, the forests are mixed and they contain a wide array of different species in a single area. The rainforests are somewhat limited and pure stands are few. In the more mountainous parts of the country, you can find subtropical species—tall grasses, weeds, bamboo, and brushwood invade the logged areas and grow all around the modern settlements, as well as along the railroads and arterial highways. In between the upland forests and logged areas, you will find a mixture of all forest types.

Some areas of Vietnam are densely forested. This is Cat Ba National Park.

Pygmy slow loris can be found in the east of the Mekong River region.

RESEARCH PROJECT

Create a map that shows the major waterways in the country of Vietnam and also mark where the major cities are located.

TEXT-DEPENDENT QUESTIONS

1. What bodies of water are along the coast of Vietnam?

2. What is the climate like in the northern regions of Vietnam?

3. What Vietnamese species relies on this region as a large part of conservation efforts?

A mother and child in traditional Vietnamese dress in Mu Cang Chai in Yen Bai Province.

missionary: an individual who is sent on a mission; frequently a person who helps to promote Christianity in a foreign country

reunification: the restoration of the political unity of a specific group or place, especially in an area that was previously a formally divided territory

sortie: a sudden issuing of troops from a defensive position against the enemy

CHAPTER 2

THE GOVERNMENT & HISTORY OF VIETNAM

Vietnam is a country with a diverse history that has received much of its modern influence from China. With a past that includes quite a bit of conflict and slow economic growth, the nation continues to develop.

For many years, the rule of Vietnam was fought over, with the Chinese and the French playing significant roles in the history of the country. In more modern times, Communism and the Vietnam War have shaped the country into what it is today.

From prehistoric times to modern-day Vietnam, the country has struggled to overcome its past—being a poor, third-world country. Thanks to the tireless work of countless governments and ruling parties, it is expected that Vietnam will shed its third-world status very soon. This is a significant feat, and something the Vietnamese government has been working for years to achieve.

Prehistoric Vietnam

The recorded history of Vietnam can be traced all the way back to the mid-to-late part of the third century BCE. At that time, the states of Au Lac and Nanyue were established in the region.

Records have shown that prehistoric Vietnam was home to many of the world's earliest societies and civilizations. In fact, it was in this area that people first

It is thought that the cultivation of rice in Vietnam dates back to ancient times. These rice terraces have been cut into the hillside.

practiced rice cultivation and agriculture, with the Red River Delta creating an all-natural geographic and economic unit. The land was bounded to the west and north by jungles and mountains, to the south by the Red River Delta, and to the east by the sea.

It is believed that the very first state in Vietnam was founded in the year 2879 BCE; however, more recent archaeological studies have suggested a development toward chiefdoms that occurred during the latter part of the Bronze Age, in the Dong Son culture.

The Bronze Age: Dong Son Culture

By approximately 300 BCE, a new civilization with very elaborate arts based on working in bronze existed and extended all the way from the Tonkin region into Indonesia, Cambodia, Laos and, of course, Vietnam. While this is called the Dong Son culture, there are some who believe it was not actually a cultural unity. Several bronze ritual works were discovered that were cast using the lost-wax method (an ancient casting technique). Some were decorated with animal and human figures with masks. The main objects that they made were ceremonial drums, a skill that spread to other countries in the region.

Due to the peculiar geography of Vietnam, it was challenging to attack. This is why the country remained a self-contained and independent state under the Hung kings for such a long time.

Invasion of the Chinese Dynasties: 111 BCE–938 CE

While Vietnam was difficult to invade and attack, it did eventually succumb to the rule of foreign entities. For more than 1,100 years, from 111 BCE to 938 CE, the country was governed by several different Chinese dynasties, including the Han, the Eastern Wu, the Jin, the Liu Song, the Southern Qi, the Liang, the Sui, the Tang, and

A Dong Son bronze drum copy. The original ancient drums were used as a musical instrument in ritual ceremonies.

the Southern Han. During this time, in addition to developing the horticulture system that mainly fueled the economy, there were artisans from the urban area of Dai La who mastered crucial skills, such as iron casting, copper casting and molding, and goldsmith work. The literate people in Dai La began using Chinese characters when writing, but they were not often recorded, as historians did not exist during this time.

The change of rule from Vietnamese to Chinese led to the loss of the native Vietnamese culture, language, heritage, and, in a large part, the nation's identity. During certain periods of the 1,100 year occupation of China, Vietnam was governed independently by the Duong Dinh Nge, Khucs, Early Lys, Trung Sisters, and Trieus, but each of these groups' reigns were only temporary. In particular, the Trung Sisters's courage and exploits are legendary, with Trung Nhi and Trung Nhac being daughters of the local Lac lord. It is believed they opted to commit suicide rather than submit to the Chinese.

A procession of elephan
memory of the Trung Si
in Saigon in 1957.

Lac Long Quan was a Hung king of the Hong Bang dynasty of ancient Vietnam. This is the site of his tomb.

The Hong Bang Dynasty

In reference to a legend that was first seen in the Linh Nam chich quai ("Selection of Strange Tales in Linh Nam"), a fourteenth-century book, Loc Tuc, the tribal chief, founded the state of Xich Quy in the year 2879 BCE and named himself Kinh Duong Vuong, which started the period called Hong Bang.

Kinh Duong Vuong's successor was Sung Lam, and the following line of ancient Vietnamese kings called themselves the Hung kings and renamed the country "Van Lang." This is thought to have been a matriarchal society, which was common in the Pacific Islands and Southeast Asia during this time.

After a total of eighteen generations of the Hung kings, the country of Van Lang finally fell to an invasion by the An Duong Vuong in 258 BCE.

Early Historical Periods: Enter the Europeans

The very first Portuguese sailors reached Da Nang on the coast of Vietnam in the year 1516 CE. They were followed by a party of Dominican **missionaries**. In the following decades, the Vietnamese and Portuguese began to trade and set up a commercial colony.

Eventually, the Catholic Church had a huge impact on Vietnam. In fact, its influence here was more than on any other Asian country, besides the Philippines.

Tay Son Rebellion

In the year 1765, a rebellion occurred in the town of Tay Son, which is located near Quy Nhon. The rebels of this area were led by the Nguyen brothers, who controlled

Nha Trang Cathedral is the principal church of Catholic diocese of Nha Trang.

The tomb of King Thieu Tri in Hue. Hue was the seat of the Nguyen dynasty.

entral Vietnam for over a decade. In 1783, the city of Saigon was captured from the guyen lords. During the rebellion, the Chinese moved to take advantage of the tuation, but the Nguyen brothers were successful with their rebellion efforts.

Enter the French:
887–1954

ilitary activity in Vietnam by the French began in 1847 when the French Navy tacked the Da Nang harbor in a response to the suppression of Catholic issionaries by Emperor Thieu Tri. In 1859, Saigon was seized by the French and e region received the name Cochinchina, which was made up by three eastern ovinces of Vietnam. The rest of the country was divided into two other parts: nkin and Annam.

The French remained in control for many years, providing Vietnam with many new cultural elements that are seen in the history of the country from this point forward. In fact, each ruling entity left its mark on the country, creating a very diverse heritage when it comes to the people of this country.

Ba Na Hills village dates back to 1919. It was originally a resort for French colonists.

Modern History: The Effects of WWII

In 1940, France fell to Nazi Germany and the Indochinese government acquiesced to the presence of the Japanese troops that were in Vietnam. At this point, the Japanese allowed the French administration to continue running the country. Also at this time, the country was spared the many ravages that occurred in other countries during the Japanese occupation, and things ran as normal.

However, near the end of the war, several circumstances melded together to create a disaster. The Japanese rice requisitions, along with floods and breaches that occurred in the dikes, led to a famine that struck most of the 10 million people in North Vietnam. Many starved to death. At this time, the U.S. government only assisted to a limited extent.

Warring with the French

Through all the turmoil with the Japanese, the French eventually managed to regain control of Vietnam. But when Haiphong was shelled by the French in 1946, killing civilians, fighting broke out in Hanoi. This started the Franco-Viet Minh War. After eight years of fighting, the Viet Minh had gained control of most of Laos, and

Learn about the infamous Ho Chi Minh, Vietnam's future revolutionary in this captivating video.

eventually the French troops surrendered. This surrender was short-lived, however, as the whole country believed they would be liberated. Unfortunately, very different political beliefs existed in the northern and southern parts of this country, which eventually led to a formal division of the northern and the southern portions of Vietnam.

The Separation of Vietnam

After the Geneva Accords were sealed and the French agreed to withdraw their troops from northern Vietnam, the South became a separate nation from the North, being ruled by the Ngo Dinh Diem government. At this time, the southern portion of the country was rocked by the anti-Diem unrest, and then the United States determined that Diem was a liability and supported the military coup.

At the same time, the northern part of Vietnam was put under the rule of Hanoi, and the new government eliminated any members of the population that threatened the government.

The North-South War

Efforts to help liberate the South of Vietnam (which were eventually named the Vietnam War) began in 1959. Hanoi formed the National Liberation Front (NLF), which eventually earned the title "Viet Cong." American soldiers nicknamed these forces "Charlie."

After the NLF's campaign was launched, the Diem government began to lose control of the countryside. The battle between the North and the South raged, and other countries quickly began to get involved, including America.

The Coming of the Cavalry

The United States saw the colonial war in Indochina (Vietnam) as an important worldwide fight against the expansion of communism.

The Gulf of Tonkin Incident

One of the most decisive turnin points in the U.S. strategy against Vietnam occurred in 1964 in what was referred to as the Gulf of Tonkin Incident. Over the course of several days, two U.S. destroyers, the *Turner Joy* and the *Maddox*, made the claim they had been victims of unprovoked attacks while sailing along the North Vietnamese coast.

After further research, it was proved that provocation was present—the initial attack occurred when the *Maddox* was in North Vietnamese waters helping a commando of South Vietnam in a raid. Even though the attack was proven to be provoked, President Johnson ordered sixty-four sorties to rain bombs on the North. However, the two aircraft ordered for this attack were lost and the first American prisoner of war (POW) was captured. After this battle, the United States passed the Tonkin Gulf Resolution, giving the president the ability to take any measures to repel attack against United States forces to prevent any further aggression.

Walt Whitman Rostow shows President Lyndon B. Johnson a model of the Khe Sanh area in February 1968.

ietnam was considered to be the next Communist domino to fall. The U.S. Military
ssistance Advisory Group (MAAG) entered Vietnam in 1950, and there were
merican troops present in the country for the next twenty-five years.

By January of 1968, the Vietnamese troops in the North began a major attack
long the Vietnamese Demilitarized Zone, in Khe Sanh. As the biggest attack of the
ntire war, it was crafted by the North to take attention off another strategy called the
et Offensive, which included attacks on more than 100 cities.

During the Vietnam War, Richard M. Nixon was elected president, in part for
s promise to have a secret to end the war. This secret turned out to be the "Nixon
octrine," which was released in 1969. It called on Asian countries to become more
elf-reliant in measures of defense. The strategy Nixon had created was for
etnamization, which meant the South would have to fight the battle on their own,
ithout the help of the U.S. military.

The Vietnam War lasted through President Kennedy's and Lyndon B.
hnson's terms of office, and into Richard Nixon's. Other countries besides the

United States that were heavily involved in the Vietnam War included Thailand, the Philippines, South Korea, New Zealand, and Australia, which made this battle truly a worldwide battle on Vietnam soil.

The South's Fall and the Reunification of Vietnam

In 1973, the United States left Vietnam, and in 1975, the North launched a huge ground attack that ended the war. On the initial day of the North's victory, Saigon's name was changed to Ho Chi Minh City; however, this was just the first of many changes to come. The formal **reunification** of Vietnam occurred in July of 1976, and the South fell under the rule of the Provisional Revolutionary Government.

The Reunification Palace in Ho Chi Minh City was the home and workplace of the President of South Vietnam during the Vietnam War.

Modern Vietnam

While relations between Vietnam and other countries have improved over the years, there is still discord. In addition to improving relations with the United States, Vietnam has also improved relations with the country's historic conqueror, China. While Vietnam is still overshadowed by China in many ways, the economic boom it has seen has led to rapid growth and development.

Today, Vietnam is a member of ASEAN (the Association of Southeast Asian Nations), a group of ten Southeast Asian countries that came together in a shared fear of communism. Nowadays, though, the organization promotes intergovernmental cooperation and facilitates economic, political, security, military, educational, and sociocultural integration, Vietnam's economy is growing at a rate of more than 8 percent per year.

RESEARCH PROJECT

Give a two-minute presentation on one of the Chinese dynasties that ruled Vietnam.

TEXT-DEPENDENT QUESTIONS

1. What was the Gulf of Tonkin Incident?

2. What was the Nixon Doctrine and how did it affect Vietnam?

3. When did the Vietnam War finally end?

capitalism: a political and economic system where a country's industry and trade are controlled by the private sector with the aim of profit, instead of by the state

Gross Domestic Product: a monetary measure of the market value of all final goods and services produced in a country during a period of time; commonly used to determine the economic performance of a country and to make international comparisons

per capita income: the average income per person in a given location during the course of a certain year

CHAPTER 3

THE VIETNAMESE ECONOMY

Vietnamese Economy While Governed by Others

For centuries, Vietnam's economy was built on farming, particularly by producing rice along the fertile Red River Delta plains of northern Vietnam. It was not until the tenth century that Vietnam began to acquire land to the south in order to grow more rice and form more villages.

In the nineteenth century, Vietnam fell under the colonial rule of France, which split Vietnam into two sections—the North and the South—with plans to develop them separately. In the eyes of the French, the North was suited for agriculture (rice production), while the South had natural resources (coal production) that could be exported to other countries. After the Vietnam War, the country experienced little economic growth.

Today, however, Vietnam is a successful exporter, and those activities fuel good economic growth in the country. However, the nation still has a way to go to fully create an advanced market economy that fits in with the rest of the world. As of 2017, Vietnam's **Gross Domestic Product** (GDP) was $223.9 billion USD and the **per capita income** was $802.00. Overall, Vietnam's economic freedom score is 53.1, meaning it's the one hundred and forty first freest economy as of 2018.

Under the Chinese: 111 BCE–938 CE

During the time of Chinese occupation, the Chinese developed the horticulture system that mainly fueled the economy, and also taught the people living there Chinese techniques of dike construction and how to care and breed domestic animals. These new activities bolstered economic growth.

Under the French: 1887–1954

France colonized Vietnam for economic exploitation. They formed a Western-style government that ruled every sector of administration and left little, if any, power to

The Chinese introduced horticulture into Vietnam during its occupation.

A Vietnamese worker in a food-processing factory.

The Economy of Vietnam

Gross Domestic Product (GDP):
$223.86 billion USD

Industries:
mobile phones, tires, glass, chemical fertilizer, cement, steel, coal, mining, machine-building, shoes, textiles, garments, food processing

Agriculture:
rice, tea, sugarcane, rubber, peanuts, cotton, coffee

Export Commodities:
processed forest products, aquaculture, coal, rubber, coffee, rice, garments and textiles, crude oil

Export Partners:
US 20.1%, China 14.5%, Japan 8%, South Korea 6.8% (2017)

Import Commodities:
machinery and equipment, petroleum products, steel products, raw materials for the clothing and shoe industries, electronics, plastics, automobiles

Import Partners:
China 25.8%, South Korea 20.5%, Japan 7.8%, Thailand 4.9%

Currency:
Dong

Source: www.cia.gov 2017

the Vietnamese. In fact, those emperors who opposed France's rule were deposed and replaced with those who welcomed French rule. Some Vietnamese still held positions in government, but these were largely low-level, low-paying positions.

Economic policies initiated by Paul Doumer, France's president at the time, sought to develop French Indochina, as it was called. France was not interested in industrial development in Vietnam, but instead sought to consume and export the country's resources. To do so, during the occupation, France built highways, railroads, bridges, canals, and other public works to bring forth rapid expansion.

Tourism in Vietnam

Vietnam is an astonishingly beautiful country, so it is not surprising that tourism today is now an important component of the modern Vietnamese economy. However, when compared to other southeast Asian countries, tourism has been slow to start. Even though the war ended decades ago, its effects have been long-lasting. Unexploded mines and land poisoned by chemicals have held tourism back. Despite this, Vietnam now attracts millions of tourists each year, bringing vital foreign exchange into the country.

The French colonial government received funds through local taxes and by trading opium, salt, rice, and alcohol. This made up about 44 percent of the country's budget until the 1920s, when the economy began to change. Once the auto industry developed in France at the turn of the century, rubber was in great need. For this reason, France developed the rubber industry in Indochina by creating rubber plantations. This made France a leading producer of rubber and resulted in more investment in Vietnam by firms such as Michelin, which still sells rubber tires today.

From there, Vietnam began to industrialize and produce tea, coffee, textiles, beer, tobacco, and cement to be exported throughout the French Empire.

Unfortunately, the aim was immediate financial gain for investors rather than the economic development of Vietnam. In fact, a very small percentage of profits gained through exports were reinvested back into Vietnam's economy.

All in all, the economic progress of Vietnam during this time only benefited France and a small class of elite Vietnamese. Although much rice was being produced in the land by peasant farmers—many of whom had to pay rent to a landowner—most of the rice was exported. The Vietnamese people struggled to feed the masses with the little rice that was left over. This form of **capitalism** was associated with foreign rule and seen by the Vietnamese as unfair. While the French continued to profit financially from the colonial rule of Vietnam, the people of

The Presidential Palace is located in the city of Hanoi. It was built between 1900 and 1906 to house the French Governor-General of Indochina.

Vietnam did not profit economically. This view of foreign rule meshed with capitalism gave rise to national resistance movements.

Vietnamese Economy While Self-Governing

Since 1954, Vietnam's economy has been transitioning from a centrally planned, agricultural economy to an economy based on industry with a free market. Even today, approximately 40 percent of the total population still works in agriculture.

Although suffering from debt problems, Vietnam is viewed as of one of Asia's successes. This growth has improved the living standards of its population.

Vietnam's government is committed to developing the country's economy into a stable, low inflation one with a sizable manufacturing sector. However, like many

Vietnamese women mending fishing nets in a repair shop. Fishing is an important part of Vietnam's economy.

Learn more about the emerging economic boom in Vietnam.

countries around the world Vietnam did suffer from the global financial crisis of 2007-2008. Fortunately for Vietnam, it was one of the few southeast Asian emerging economies not to have gone into recession in the wake of this world economic crisis.

Today, Vietnam's commitment to trade and integration with the rest of the world has helped it to overcome many of its earlier problems.

In the realm of monetary stability, growth has been somewhat high and steady over the past ten years, while inflation has been somewhat controlled. The Vietnamese Dong, the national currency, is a closed currency and is pegged to the dollar in the United States. However, the state bank in Vietnam is slowly working to implement measures that will free up the banking system to prepare for monetary reform.

A worker in a clothing factory in Hanoi. Manufacturing for export is on the increase in Vietnam.

Taxes and Other Income

In January of 2009, Vietnam reformed its entire tax system to adapt the regulatory system to the country's thriving economic development. The old legislation regarding taxation was replaced by the Enterprise Income Tax Law, which affects business owners in Vietnam. In this country, there are several different sources of law that govern different tax types for businesses: the Enterprise Income Tax Law, and for individuals, the Personal Income Tax Law.

The General Department of Taxation is under the Ministry of Finance in Vietnam, which is where the tax authorities work. Due to the recent economic growth in Vietnam, it has become an extremely popular area for those looking to invest in citizenship by making payments to the government, which has helped to further grow the country's economic and development sectors.

The Labor Force

In 2016, the labor force in Vietnam was reported to be at almost 56 million people. The labor force is made up of people who are fifteen years of age or older. Some of the hottest jobs and most popular careers for individuals in Vietnam today include nursing, running tea shops, production jobs, manufacturing, and shoe repair. With the expanding economy, the number of professional industries in Vietnam is growing, which in turn is opening up new opportunities for the relatively young workforce. These new opportunities are providing more lucrative positions for those in the area and ensuring they can pursue the career they are most passionate about.

Economic Sectors of Vietnam

Prior to the early 1990s, Vietnam was involved in various conflicts across its borders, the last one being a series of border clashes with China. Once the war was over, Vietnam's economic structure changed significantly. The result was a decline of the agricultural industry, which previously made up a total of 40.8 percent of the GDP in the year 1989, to just 27.1 percent in the year 1999. Industry in Vietnam has grown in importance, with a contribution to the GDP from

The Ministry of Construction is responsible for state-run building projects.

22.9 percent in 1989 up to 36.7 percent by 1999. During 1989–1999, the contribution of the service sector in this country remained unchanged, holding steady at 36 percent.

Even though there were significant structural changes, the country of Vietnam is still considered to have an agricultural economy regarding employment. Approximately 72 percent of the labor force in Vietnam, which represents 28 million people, works in the agricultural industry.

With the Doi Moi ("Renovation") Policy that was introduced in 1986, as well as the Vietnamese goal to reduce the public sector's size, starting in the latter part of

Despite recent changes, Vietnam is still considered to have a largely agricultural economy.

Teachers are employed by the public sector in Vietnam.

the 1990s, the state sector only employed approximately 9 percent of Vietnam's total labor force, which was 39 million. The service sector in Vietnam is made up of those in the government sector, which includes teachers. Other careers fall into the retail trade sector, a growing tourist industry, and an ever-expanding banking and finance sector.

Transportation

The transportation situation in Vietnam lags behind many of the transport systems of its neighboring countries. However, it is improving as the country advances economically. However, there is still a long way to go and even today the main method by which goods are transported is by barge. The traffic is on Vietnam's roadways is very congested, dangerous, and extremely slow to travel due to the outdated design and the inappropriate mix of traffic present. In recent years, the government has launched a program to build expressways. Air travel is also

A Vietjet Air Airbus airplane landing at Tan Son Nhat International Airport in Ho Chi Minh City. Vietjet is a low-cost airline.

important in Vietnam, however, but unfortunately, many of its airports are outdated and its state-run airline is in great need of investment. Recently, however, the carrier has started to buy new state-of-the-art airplanes including the Boeing 787-9 and the Airbus A350. Vietnam has three important international airports, Noi Bai Airport in Hanoi and Tan Son Nhat Airport in Ho Chi Minh City. A third airport, Da Nang Airport, in Da Nang, also accepts some international flights.

Vietnam's railway system is old but dependable and is often one of the best ways of getting around the country. Apart from the Ho Chi Minh City–Hanoi run, there are three other lines linking Hanoi with the other parts of Vietnam. The first runs east to the port city of Haiphong. A second heads northeast to Lang Son and continues across the border to Nanning in China. A third runs northwest to Lao Cai.

New metro systems are now being constructed in the two main metropolises, Ho Chi Minh City and Hanoi.

In Vietnam, the length of the entire road system is 138,055 miles (222,179 km) with 19 percent of it paved—meaning 81 percent of the roads in Vietnam are dirt roads. The money for the construction and maintenance of roadways comes from several sources, including business organizations, overseas donors, and the government. Vietnamese roads are classified based on their administrative hierarchy, with each class being assigned an abbreviation and a milestone color:

- National roads: managed by the central government and marked with white milestones that have red tops
- Freeways or expressways: marked by black on yellow indicators that are on direction signs
- Provincial roads: managed by the individual provinces and are marked by a white milestone with a green or blue top
- District roads: managed by the rural district and marked with white milestones that have brown tops
- Commune roads: managed by the communes
- Urban roads: managed by individual towns and cities

The roads in Ho Chi Minh City are often congested and dangerous.

Energy

The main source of commercial energy in Vietnam is petroleum, which is responsible for contributing approximately 25 percent of the country's total energy. The oil reserves in the country are estimated to be at 600 million tons. In 2004, oil production increased rapidly and peaked at 403,300 barrels per day, but this has steadily declined. Crude oil was the top export from Vietnam until the latter part of the 2000s, which is when the high-tech electrical manufacturers began to emerge as the main export market.

In 2015, renewable energy including biomass and hydro together contributed about 25 percent of the total primary energy supply. At the same time, coal share has grown from 15 percent in 2000 to 35 percent of total supply in 2015. Unfortunately for the environment, this trend is expected to continue into the future as the domestic supply of hydro and biomass seems to be unable to meet the increasing demand.

Bac Lieu wind power plant in the Mekong Delta offers clean energy for Vietnam.

Financial and business centers of Ho Chi Minh City.

RESEARCH PROJECT

Provide a one-page overview of the main imports and exports of Vietnam.

TEXT-DEPENDENT QUESTIONS

1. What existing well-known tire company was one of the first to invest in the Vietnamese rubber industry?

2. How many people still work in the agriculture industry today?

3. What percentage of roads are paved in Vietnam?

Muong girls wearing traditional dress during the Lunar New Year holiday in Ha Giang Province.

WORDS TO UNDERSTAND

Confucianism: a system of ethical and philosophical teachings that were originally founded by Confucius and then developed by Mencius, an early Chinese philosopher

Francophonie, the: an international organization representing locations where French is a primary or customary language

Indochina: relating to or constituting a large language family that covers mainland Southeast Asia, along with scattered areas throughout Nepal, India, Bangladesh, and the Chinese southern border

CHAPTER 4

CITIZENS OF VIETNAM—PEOPLE, CUSTOMS & CULTURE

Located on the most eastern tip of the **Indochina** peninsula in the region of Southeast Asia, the country of Vietnam is one of the largest and most densely populated countries in the entire area. While precise population figures for Vietnam are difficult to obtain, it is estimated that in 2018, 96.49 million people reside there, which has increased from the 2012 estimate of 91.5 million. This makes Vietnam the fourteenth most populated country in the world.

As a diverse country, more people are migrating to this part of the world today than ever before. With many of the country's modern cultural aspects coming from its neighbor, China, the Vietnamese people have maintained a sense of Chinese tradition within their country. Today, there are countless appealing attractions in the country that people flock to year after year, and tourism strongly contributes to the growing economy of Vietnam.

Ethnicities

Vietnam is a country that's considered multiethnic, with more than fifty distinct ethnic groups. Currently, there are fifty-four ethnicities that the Vietnamese government has officially recognized, each one having a unique cultural heritage, lifestyle, and language. Quite a few of the local ethnic groups living in the mountain regions are collectively referred to as Degar. They are also known as "Montagnard," which is a leftover French word that means "people of the mountain."

The largest ethnic populations in Vietnam include Kinh at 85.7 percent, Tay at 1.9 percent, Tai Ethnic at 1.8 percent, Muong at 1.5 percent, Khmer Krom at 1.5 percent, Mong at 1.2 percent, Nung at 1.1 percent, and Hoa at one percent. A mixture of many different ethnic groups make up the remaining 4.3 percent.

In Vietnam there are minority ethnic groups who inhabit the highland regions. It is interesting that they are always colorfully dressed in traditional costume while they go about their daily lives.

A Muong woman in traditional dress. The Muong inhabit the mountainous region in the north of the country.

Learn more about Vietnamese culture in this fast-paced video.

Language

In Vietnam, the official and national language is Vietnamese, and most of the population speaks it. It is an Austroasiatic language and has origins in the northern part of the country. Initially, Vietnamese was created using modified Chinese characters; however, at a later time, the natives of Vietnam created their own script, which was called Chu Nom. Not only is Vietnamese spoken in Vietnam, it's also heard in other parts of the world where a large number of former Vietnam residents have relocated.

In addition to the main language, Tay is also present in this country, typically spoken in the north, close to the Chinese border. Some of the other minority languages found in Vietnam include: Khmer, Cham, Muong, Chinese, Nung, and Mong.

When it comes to foreign languages, French is the most common. With a legacy of colonial rule, there is a large population of Vietnamese people who speak French as a second language, and Vietnam is a full member of the **Francophonie** since French was once its main language. There are also small sectors of the Vietnamese population who speak Polish, German, Czech, and Russian, with English gaining recent popularity.

Religion in Vietnam

Vietnam has a long history, and as a result, many religions exist in the country. The main religions include Vietnamese folk religion—historically structured under **Confucianism** doctrines—and Taoism, both of which are derived from China. There's also a strong Buddhist tradition in Vietnam, which is called the "Three Teachings" when paired with Confucianism and Taoism.

Food and Drink

The food in Vietnam is notable due to its fresh and flavorful ingredients. Throughout the country, a wide array of regional variations exists; however, one thing that's similar across the country is the fact that noodles or rice typically form the base of any Vietnamese meal. Fish is plentiful, and there is a huge reliance on fresh vegetables and herbs in addition to shrimp paste and fermented fish sauce. Generally, Vietnamese cuisine is considered very healthy.

The national drink in Vietnam is green tea, which is something that accompanies virtually every social gathering and business meal, and is typically drunk after all meals. At the other end of the spectrum, the Vietnamese also consume rice wine frequently; however, they also have local beer, as well as a huge selection of imported spirits and wines.

A Vietnamese girl praying in a Buddhist temple in Ho Chi Minh City.

Official statistics from the Vietnamese government state that more than 24 million people out of the total population of more than 90 million identify with one of the recognized, organized religions. Of all these people, about 11 million are Buddhists, while 6.2 million are Catholics, 4.4 million Caodaists, 1.4 million Protestants, and 1.3 million Hoahaoists. Smaller religious groups are thriving in Vietnam as well, including 1,500 Hindus, 7,000 Bahais, and 75,000 Muslims. The traditional folk religions in Vietnam that practice ancestor worship, along with venerating many goddesses and gods, have experienced a significant rebirth since the early portion of the 1980s.

Education

The education system in Vietnam is managed by the state and includes both private and public education facilities run by the Ministry of Education and Training. There are five distinct levels to the education system: preschool, primary and secondary school, high school, and finally, higher education. A person who has a formal education is defined as having twelve total years of "basic education." Basic education in Vietnam is defined as five years in primary school, followed by four years in intermediate schooling and three total years of secondary education. Most basic education students only attend school for half of a day.

Vietnam is well known for a rigorous curriculum that is considered extremely competitive. By the time children reach the secondary education levels, they can choose to apply to various "High Schools for the Gifted," which are extremely prestigious and often require very high exam scores.

A teacher with her students at a village school in Kien Giang Province in the Mekong Delta region.

Football (Soccer) is a popular sport in Vietnam. These kids from Binh Thuan Province are enjoying a practice session.

To gain entrance into a university, a student must score above a certain level on the National High School Graduation Examination. The higher a score a student achieves, the more prestigious the institution they are able to attend. In Vietnam, those who are not able to pass the graduation exam are often looked down on by other members of society.

Sports

Sports in Vietnam are diverse, and the Vietnamese people participate in a wide array of team athletics. Football, one of the main sports and considered the most popular, is managed by the Vietnam Football Federation.

People in Vietnam also play Australian Rules Football, which is a sport that was first adopted in 1998. Other popular athletic endeavors in Vietnam include cricket, rugby union, badminton, tennis, chess, martial arts, and running.

Vietnamese Martial Arts

As one of the most popular sports in Vietnam, the country's style of martial arts has quite a few international followers. In fact, the sport has been adopted in more than 100 countries. However, the actual origins of Vietnamese martial arts went past moral refinement and health training—the characteristics in the majority of sports games played today. Martial arts of Vietnam were created to protect the royal family, along with the entire nation. Although there are several types of Vietnamese martial arts, the two most popular that are still practiced today include Vo Kinh and Viet Vo Dao.

Kids learning a Vietnamese martial art at school in Ho Chi Minh City.

The One Pillar Pagoda is a historic Buddhist site built in 1049 by King Ly Thai Tong.

The Arts: Architecture, Painting, Music, and Literature

The arts, along with architecture in the Southeast Asia region, have significant influences from China, India, and other traditions from nearby countries. Hinduism had a significant impact on the region during the country's early history; however, in later centuries, Buddhism grew in popularity and has remained the focal point of life in this region. This is why the majority of arts and architecture in Vietnam has very strong ties to Buddhism.

Ancient Houses in Hoi An in Quang Nam Province. It is a UNESCO world heritage site.

When it comes to performing arts, the most famous in Vietnam is called "water puppetry." This tradition originally evolved during the eleventh century in the Red River Delta. Each year, the river flooded the lowlands, offering the ideal platform to conceal the puppeteers, along with their poles, and provided the mechanics for the puppets' movements. During the Vietnam War, exhibitions of water puppetry became scarce, but thanks to the increase in tourism to the region, shows are now performed regularly again.

An ancient form of theater called Cheo has been present in Vietnam since the Bronze Age, which is obvious from the depictions of the performances that have been found on drums in that region. The word "cheo" is derived from the Chinese word that means "laughter," and the art is made up of an improvised, comical performance that includes traditional instruments.

Traditional music in Vietnam is divided into two basic categories—dieu nam in the southern regions and dieu bac in the northern areas. The southern style of music

Traditional Vietnamese water puppet theater show.

A Vietnamese craftswoman making traditional bamboo fish traps in Thu Sy village in Hung Yen Province.

is closely related to Chinese music, while northern music has been influenced by th indigenous Cham culture.

In recent years, handicrafts from the local villages have seen a resurgence, with entire villages now recognized for creating a signature craft, such as silk, conical hats, parasols, pottery, and lacquer ware. Today, there are approximately 2,500 different craft villages throughout Vietnam, all with the goal of preserving the cultural heritage of the country.

Traditional Vietnamese Lacquer ware.

RESEARCH PROJECT

Write a one-page essay on the history and development of martial arts throughout southeast Asia.

TEXT-DEPENDENT QUESTIONS

1. What is the primary language spoken in Vietnam?

2. What is the most popular sport in Vietnam?

3. What is the name of an ancient type of theater present in Vietnam?

The Ho Chi Min
City skyline and
the Saigon Rive

Dragon King: a Chinese water and weather god, also known as the Dragon God

napalm: a highly flammable sticky jelly used in incendiary bombs and flamethrowers, consisting of gasoline thickened with special soaps

Sanskrit: a language of ancient India with historical documents dating back 3,500 years

CHAPTER 5

FAMOUS CITIES OF VIETNAM

Vietnam is considered one of the oldest countries in history. Throughout the years, the country has been affected by cultural influences from the Chinese, Khmer, Indian, and French. The nation has a vast war history, and also has many temples and sacred places where citizens can pay their respects to past leaders and gods. Throughout Vietnam's history, great cities have appeared that still stand today, although some of the names have been changed. Bustling, thriving cities such as Ho Chi Minh City and Da Nang have modern appeal, yet many still retain the charm of bygone days.

Ho Chi Minh City

Ho Chi Minh City, previously known as Saigon, is full of history, exotic foods, and markets that sell anything from local crafts to electronics. With a population of over 8.4 million people and over 7.4 million motorbikes zooming around, this is a busy place! The city was named after the last president of South Vietnam, Ho Chi Minh who inspired the people in the revolution, as well as started the Indochinese Communist Party.

Districts in Ho Chi Minh City

Ho Chi Ming City has twenty-four different districts of various sizes. There are nineteen city districts and five rural districts. District 1 is the central business district and the main entertainment area as well. The different districts offer different people, culture, and food.

Ben Thanh Market

One of the more popular markets is the Ben Thanh Market located in District 1. Featuring over 3,000 stalls, the market offers fruits, vegetables, and all the dry goods one needs. There are also many stalls that sell a variety of T-shirts and souvenirs for tourists to remember some of the special attractions they visited, as well as pictures of beautiful scenery that they saw on their vacation.

Tan Dinh Market

Also located in District 1, Tan Dinh Market specializes in selling silks and delicate clothing materials. This market has more of the finer goods and foods to offer than some of the other markets. Tan Dinh Market was considered "The

War Remnants Museum

Located in District 3, the War Remnants Museum contains more than 20,000 documents, films, and exhibits to share with the public relating to the "American War" and the first Indochina War involving the French colonialists. The museum has had over 15 million visitors in the past thirty-five years and has become one of the most visited places in Ho Chi Minh City. Several themed rooms allow tourists to explore different aspects of the war, including a walled yard containing some of the military equipment used during these wars. For example, they have a UH-1 Huey helicopter, a BLU-82 Daisy Cutter bomb, an F-5A fighter jet, an M48 Patton tank, a Douglas A-1 Skyraider attack bomber, and an A-37 Dragonfly attack bomber. To make it more exciting spread throughout the equipment in the yard are several intact explosive devices, but their fuses and charges have been removed for safety reasons.

There is a building that contains "tiger cages," which is where the South Vietnamese kept their political prisoners. There are some exhibits with graphic photography of all sorts of past events that are not suitable for all ages and stomachs. One building shows the effects of napalm and phosphorus bombs, while another has an actual guillotine last used to execute prisoners in 1960 by the French and South Vietnamese.

Pearl of the Far East" during the Saigon days because of the higher brand names that were sold there—and are still sold there to this day. As well as serving the famous delicious Vietnamese Pancake, the market offers some exotic foods for the daring type such as snails, pork brains, fermented pork rolls, and ruou ran (snake wine).

Hanoi

Hanoi is one of the most ancient cities in the world, with documents dating back to 2000 BCE. Today Hanoi is the capital of Vietnam and the country's second largest city by population. Hanoi is located next to the Red River, a little more than 1,000 miles north of Ho Chi Minh City. On October 10, 2010, the city celebrated its 1,000th anniversary by reenacting numerous past events and having a big parade.

Ben Thanh Market in Ho Chi Minh City is a great place to buy a great range of goods and souvenirs.

Located in Hanoi, the Ho Chi Minh Mausoleum serves as the resting place of Vietnam's revolutionary leader Ho Chi Minh.

Ho Cho Minh Mausoleum

Located in the Ba Dinh Square, this building is a favorite tourist attraction in Hanoi. Here lies former President Ho Chi Minh, one of the most idolized and popular leaders of Vietnam. His body is well preserved in a glass case for visitors near and far to come and pay their respects.

Hoan Kiem Lake

The name of this body of water means "Lake of the Returned Sword," or "Lake of the Restored Sword." The legend that accompanies it makes it one of the most traveled scenic spots in Hanoi. The legend goes that Le Loi King found some shiny metal one day while visiting a friend. His friend caught it fishing, and not needing it, he gave the metal to Le Loi. Once home, Le Loi molded the shiny metal into a sword. After the sword was finished, the words "Thuan Thien" (Harmonious Heaven) suddenly appeared on the sword. That was when Le Loi knew it was a gift from heaven and used it in many battles.

In 1498, after many victories against the Chinese, Vietnam and China were finally at peace. One day the king was out on a boat when suddenly a turtle swam up to the boat shouting, "Please return the sword to the **Dragon King!**" Without hesitation, the king threw the sword into the lake. The turtle grabbed the sword by the mouth and dove into the water.

That is how the lake's name was changed from Thuy Quan to Hoan Kiem. Since the turtle is considered a sacred animal in Vietnamese culture, Hoan Kiem is considered a holy place that nurtures them.

Sapa

Sapa is a small mountain town that has one of the best habitats to grow Vietnam's "white gold," otherwise known as rice. Located here is the beautiful Hoang Lien Son mountain range, which includes Fan Si Pan, the country's highest peak. Thanks to

The beautiful Hoan Kiem Lake has an interesting building in the center called the Turtle Tower.

Sapa's weathered rocks and mountainous cliffs, the soil is fertile and excellent for cultivating rice. From an aerial view, the rice fields will take anyone's breath away. In September, the rice fields are bright green with patches of yellow, which signal they are getting ready for the changing of the seasons.

That rice is considered "white gold" in Vietnam has a link to the **Sanskrit** name "Dhanya" (meaning "the sustainer of the human race"). According to a folk legend, in ancient times, rice was not produced but was summoned by the desperate prayers from the people. Some say rice would suddenly appear from the heavens in the form of a ball from up above.

One legend says that one time, a large rice ball landed in the middle of the living room of an old lady while she was sweeping the floor. The rice ball and her broom happened to touch and broke into many pieces. Since then, the people of Vietnam have had to work hard with their hands to grow rice.

The town of Sapa is situated on the side of a mountain.

The attractive and ancient town of Hoi An is a popular tourist destination.

Hoi An

Not far from the more populated coastal city of Da Nang, Hoi An is more of a slow-paced city compared to the busy and more populated cities in Vietnam. Since there is no airport or train station, the only way to get there is by road. Known as being one of the most well-preserved trading posts from the fifteenth to the nineteenth century, Hoi An has many historical buildings and museums.

Since the city is not as populated as some of the other cities in Vietnam, Hoi An displays more of the Vietnamese culture and lifestyle from the point of view of the outskirts, and visitors can see how it differs from city life. When walking the streets of downtown, one will see that there are many homes with curved, sloped rooftops and brightly painted buildings. They have been around for hundreds of years!

Hoi An is famous for its special cuisine, called "Cao Lau." What makes this dish so special is that the water source for the broth is said to come from an ancient Cham well located on the outskirts of town. You know it's a special dish when the water source is in an undisclosed location!

Da Nang

Da Nang is believed to be one of the country's largest cities—after Ho Chi Minh, Hanoi, and Hai Phong. Reaching a population over 1 million in 2014, Da Nang is on its way to becoming one of the most sought-after tourist destinations in Vietnam. Located at the mouth of the Han River and coast of the South China Sea, Da Nang is considered the halfway point between Ho Chi Minh and the country's capital, Hanoi, making it a popular place for trade and markets.

Da Nang has a United States Air Force base that was active from the 1930s until 1975. Also known as the Tourane Air Base, it was a major U.S. compound where the U.S. Air Force, Marines, and Army stationed their units during the Vietnam War.

The only Dragon Bridge in the world is in Da Nang, Vietnam.

Da Nang's famous Dragon Bridge.

RESEARCH PROJECT

Write a one-page essay on four of the most sacred animals in Vietnam.

TEXT-DEPENDENT QUESTIONS

1. What is the meaning of Hoan Kiem Lake and how did the lake get its name?

2. Why is the cuisine "Cao Lau" so special?

3. What city is one of the most ancient cities in the world?

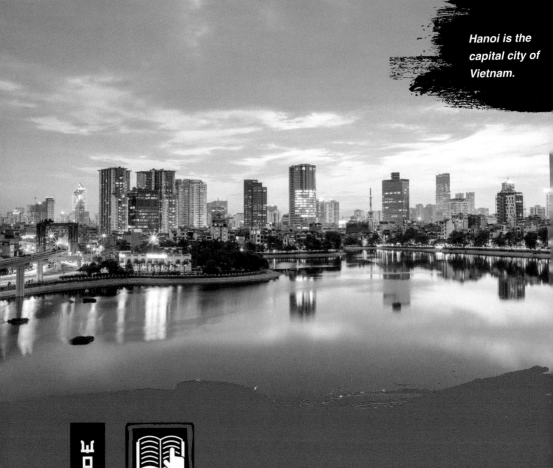

Hanoi is the capital city of Vietnam.

hydroelectricity: refers to the electricity that is generated by hydropower; the production of electrical power by using the gravitational force of flowing or falling water

market economy: an economic system where the decisions regarding distribution, production, and investment are determined by the price signals that are created by the trends of supply and demand

socialist: someone who believes in and advocates for socialism

CHAPTER 6

A BRIGHT FUTURE FOR VIETNAM

The shift of Vietnam from a centrally planned economy to a **market economy** has helped to transform the country from being one of the poorest in the entire world to a lower middle-income country. It is now considered to be one of the most dynamic emerging countries in all of the East Asia region.

With the upcoming thirty-fifth anniversary of the fall of Saigon and the fifteenth anniversary of the establishment of Vietnam-United States diplomatic relations, there's no question the country has come far; yet, it still has a long way to go. Despite a growing economy and hugely diverse population, Vietnam is still in a period of transition. However, the growth of the country is something that is inspiring for its people, as well as those on the outside looking in.

Continued Growth in Vietnam

For the past twenty-five years, Vietnam has seen explosive growth under Doi Moi from the political and economic reforms that were originally launched in 1986. Since 1990, Vietnam has had the fastest growing Gross Domestic Product (GDP) per capita in the entire world. The economy continued strengthening in 2015, when the country saw an average GDP growth rate of 6.7 percent.

Vietnam is developing a healthy export industry, producing a wide range of food products.

A significant factor attributed to the broadening of economic opportunities in Vietnam is the international integration taking place in the country. In fact, the country has signed several free trade agreements, including the Trans-Pacific Partnership, the Vietnam-EU free trade agreement, the Vietnam-Eurasia Economic Union free trade agreement among many others. Additionally, the ASEAN Economic Community was created in 2015, which is creating even more opportunities for Vietnam to further integrate with global and regional economies.

Vietnam's Economy

Vietnam has a **socialist**-oriented market economy. Currently, it is ranked number forty-seventh in the entire world, measured by the nominal GDP, and it is the thirty-fifth biggest in the world when measured by PPP (Purchasing Power Parity). Purchasing power parity is an economic theory that compares different countries' currencies through a "basket of goods" approach.

Vietnam is an active member of the World Trade Organization, ASEAN (the Association of Southeast Asian Nations), and the Asia-Pacific Economic Cooperation.

Since the mid-part of the 1980s—thanks to the reform period brought about by Doi Moi—Vietnam has made the shift away from a highly centralized command economy and is now a mixed economy, which is using both government intervention and the free market combined. As a result, the country has seen significant growth. In the twenty-first century, Vietnam is beginning to be integrated into the overall global economy.

Virtually all of the enterprises in Vietnam are small- or medium-sized enterprises. The country is a top agricultural exporter and has become an attractive destination for investment in the Southeast Asia region. Similar to other Communist countries, after the Cold War ended, Vietnam's planned economy lost its momentum for sustainable growth and productivity. Currently, the Vietnamese economy is reliant on foreign direct investment, which helps to attract capital from overseas in order to support the continued economic rigor.

Learn about Vietnam's integration into the digital economy.

The Hoa Binh Dam on the Black River is the largest hydroelectric dam in Vietnam and the second largest in Southeast Asia.

Renewable Energy in Vietnam

Vietnam has a huge opportunity ahead. They have the ability to stop relying on foreign oil and build their own modern source of renewable energy that does not pollute the waterways, agricultural land, or air.

Currently, the main source of renewable energy used in Vietnam is **hydroelectricity**. This source supplied more than 38 percent of the entire country's electricity in the year 2016. Other types of renewable energy available include solar, biomass, and wind, but these are considered marginal and account for only 0.4 percent of total electricity generation.

The Vietnamese government has plans to increase its investment in renewable energy for the purpose of energy security, as well as economic sustainability. The targets for the year 2030 include an increase in total wind power capacity to 6 gigawatts and for solar power, 12 gigawatts, from the current negligible levels. It's expected that by the year 2030, solar and wind power will account for 3.3 percent and 2.1 percent respectively of the total electricity generation.

Increased dependency on renewable energy sources will help further reduce Vietnam's reliance on third-party energy sources, which is something that's appealing to those who live in the country, as well as those in the government.

Culture

The country of Vietnam has more cultural depth than many people are aware of. While the culture of this country has been influenced significantly by China, it has been impacted by other cultures in Southeast Asia and Indonesia, as well by the French. Currently, Vietnam is the only country in Southeast Asia where the influence of Chinese predominates in dance and theater, and the culture in general. This is due to several geographical and historical factors. Vietnam was influenced by a millennium of Chinese rule affecting its politics, government, social and moral ethics, and its art forms.

In terms of geography, Vietnam belongs to the area of Southeast Asia, as well as the Indochinese Peninsula. The Kinh, who are Vietnamese people, have a huge collection of literature that includes things such as proverbs, folk ballads, and old tales. This extensive selection of written literature takes on many forms, including edicts, books, writings, and poems.

Vietnam Today and Into the Future

Vietnam is considered a dynamic and young society. One out of four people in this country's population is under the age of fourteen, and the country has a median age of just twenty-seven, with a total literacy rate of 94 percent. The labor costs in many parts of Vietnam are just half of what they are in Thailand and China.

Vietnam's government is working to provide a bright future for its young citizens by having policies to support the economy.

As Vietnam grows and develops, it will become more recognized as a highly efficient and low-cost option for factory locations for many items, including steel, rubber, oil, seafood products, shoes, textiles, and high-tech items.

As a specific percentage of the GDP, the country of Vietnam has attracted five times the foreign direct investment than what has been seen in countries such as India or China for the previous five years. In the future, large investments are predicted to fund next-generation manufacturing spanning several different industries. Many export items will be components to supply various Chinese factories.

As Vietnam grows and develops, it will become more recognized as a highly efficient and low-cost option for factory locations for many items, including steel, rubber, oil, seafood products, shoes, textiles, and high-tech items.

RESEARCH PROJECT

Create a graph that reports on renewable energy resources in Vietnam and how they affect the economy.

TEXT-DEPENDENT QUESTIONS

1. Main economic reforms have been attributed to the modern growth and progression of Vietnam. What were they called?

2. What is Vietnam's main source of renewable energy today?

3. What country has most affected and influenced the culture of Vietnam?

The main staple of the Vietnamese diet is rice, with noodles as an alternative for a snack or breakfast. In most cases, rice is accompanied by some type of meat or fish, as well as a soup and vegetable dish, and then green tea as a digestive aid. Throughout the country, people eat fish and seafood that is caught in paddy fields, the sea, canals, lakes, and rivers. The flavorings that are most commonly used include lemongrass, coriander, and shallots. Other flavors that are strongly featured include basil, anise, mint, saffron, and ginger, as well as coconut milk in the southern regions.

The most famous dish in all of Vietnam is spring rolls, which are also known as nem, nem ran, cha nem, or cha gio. Some popular combinations include crab, shrimp, or pork with rice vermicelli, bean sprouts, edible fungus, and onions rolled in rice paper wrappers and then deep fried or eaten fresh. In some situations, these are served with a bowl of lettuce, and variations also include barbecued pork strips wrapped in transparent wrappers.

Vietnamese Chicken Salad

Serves 4

Ingredients

1 tablespoon finely chopped green chili peppers
1 tablespoon rice vinegar
2 tablespoons fresh lime juice
3 tablespoons Asian fish sauce
3 cloves garlic, minced
1 tablespoon white sugar
1 tablespoon Asian (toasted) sesame oil
2 tablespoons vegetable oil
1 teaspoon black pepper
2 cooked skinless boneless chicken breast halves, shredded
½ head cabbage, cored and thinly sliced
1 carrot, cut into matchsticks
⅓ onion, finely chopped
⅓ cup finely chopped dry roasted peanuts
⅓ cup chopped fresh cilantro

Directions

1. Boil the chicken until done. Set aside to cool.

2. Stir the green chilies (chopped), peanuts, lime juice, garlic, fish sauce, rice vinegar, sugar, sesame oil, vegetable oil, and black pepper thoroughly. Be sure all the sugar has dissolved.

3. Once the chicken has cooled off, cut or tear apart the chicken into small pieces. Next, combine the cooked chicken, cabbage, carrot, onion, and cilantro and toss. Serve with dressing.

Vietnamese Chicken Wings

Serves 8

Ingredients
1 ½—2 lbs. chicken wings
8 cloves garlic, coarsely minced
¼ cup fish sauce
¼ cup sugar
3 dashes ground black pepper
1 tablespoon crushed peanuts
1 teaspoon of chilli flakes.
¼ cup cilantro, chopped

Directions
1. To start, rinse the chicken in cold water. Pat dry and place in a bowl.

2. Add the garlic, sugar, fish sauce, and black pepper. Mix well.

3. Next, add the marinade to the wings and set aside in the refrigerator for two hours, or overnight.

4. Preheat oven to 375° F. Place chicken wings on parchment paper and bake for 30 minutes. Serve immediately and top with cilantro and crushed peanuts.

Vietnamese Lettuce Wraps

Serves 8

Ingredients
1 bunch scallions, green parts only
1 head Bibb lettuce, leaves separated
  and halved through rib
4 oz. cooked thin rice noodles
8 oz. roasted pork tenderloin, cut into ¼"-
  thick slices
10 cooked medium shrimp, peeled,
  deveined, and halved lengthwise
20 tender tops of cilantro stems with
  leaves

20 mint leaves
Nuoc cham sauce for dipping

Directions
1. Boil water in a 4 quart saucepan.
Add the scallion greens and then drain
immediately. Separate the scallion
greens on paper towels and put aside.

2. Place 1 half lettuce leaf on a plate.
Add cooked noodles. Add pork and then
shrimp, and top with cilantro and mint.

3. Wrap the lettuce and then serve with
nuoc cham dipping sauce or
mayonnaise.

Vietnam festivals and holidays celebrate the culture of this country, showcasing traditions and history that have made Vietnam what it is today. Learn about some of the most important festivals and holidays celebrated in this region.

Tet Nguyen Dan

Also called the Lunar New Year, Tet takes place in January and February each year. This is the largest festival in Vietnam, with the entire country hosting family parties. Mainly a religious celebration, this isn't considered a "wild party;" however, it's still a fascinating time to visit. Locals celebrate by lighting fireworks, visiting various temples with their families, and taking in the beautiful flower stalls set up to give out flowers, which is a customary activity during Tet.

Wandering Souls Day

This festival occurs on the fifteenth day of the seventh lunar month. Locals believe the spirits of their ancestors visit their homes on this day. On the night before, families from all over go to the graves of their lost loved ones and Buddhist temples to offer fruits, sugarcane, sticky rice cakes, flowers, and prayers. Clothes and paper are usually burned during this time as well.

Even though this is another holiday celebrated by the Buddhist population, tourists can also partake in the festivities, especially in Hue where there are many Buddhist pagodas and shrines. These become flooded with monks and locals offering prayers and performing ceremonies. Another name for this particular festival is the "Cold Food Festival," with banh chay and banh troi frequently eaten.

Buddha's Birthday

In early May, Buddha's birthday is celebrated throughout Vietnam by those who are Buddhists. It occurs in the fourth lunar month and on the eighth day, with many temples adorned with extremely lavish decorations. During this time, locals offer several different Vietnamese dishes to Buddha, as well as flower garlands and fruits. The event typically draws thousands of locals and visitors who want to participate in the many activities, including parades and prayer sessions.

The Lim Festival

This occurs in the mid-part of February—during the twelfth and thirteenth day of the first lunar month. It includes UNESCO-listed Quan họ folk singing performances, along with a wide array of traditional Vietnamese games. During the festival, several different stages are built inside

Vietnamese artists performing a spiritual dance at a festival to welcome the Lunar New Year at Van Mieu (Temple of Literature) in Hanoi.

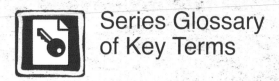

Series Glossary
of Key Terms

aboriginal	Of or relating to the original people living in a region.
archaeology	A science that deals with past human life and activities as shown by objects (as pottery, tools, and statues) left by ancient peoples.
archipelago	A group of islands.
biomass	A renewable energy source from living or recently living plant and animal materials, which can be used as fuel.
Borneo	An island of the Malay Archipelago southwest of the Philippines and divided between Brunei, Malaysia, and Indonesia.
boundary	Something that indicates or fixes a limit or extent.
Buddhism	A religion of eastern and central Asia based on the teachings of Gautama Buddha.
Christianity	A religion based on the teachings of Jesus Christ.
civilization	An advanced stage (as in art, science, and government) in the development of society.
colony	A distant territory belonging to or under the control of a nation.
commodity	Something produced by agriculture, mining, or manufacture.
Confucianism	Of or relating to the Chinese philosopher Confucius or his teachings or followers.
culture	The habits, beliefs, and traditions of a particular people, place, or time.
dialect	A form of a language that is spoken in a certain region or by a certain group.
diversity	The condition or fact of being different.
economic boom	A period of increased commercial activity within either a business, market, industry, or economy as a whole.
emerging market	An emerging market economy is a nation's economy that is progressing toward becoming advanced.
endangered species	A species threatened with extinction.
enterprise	A business organization or activity.
European Union	An economic, scientific, and political organization consisting of 27 European countries.
foreign exchange reserve	Foreign currency reserves that are held by the central bank of a country.
geothermal energy	Energy stored in the form of heat beneath the earth's surface. It is a carbon-free, renewable, and sustainable form of energy.
global warming	A warming of the earth's atmosphere and oceans that is thought to be a result of air pollution.

Hindu	A person who follows Hinduism.
Independence	The quality or state of not being under the control of, reliant on, or connected with someone or something else.
Industrialization	The widespread development of industries in a region, country, or culture.
Infrastructure	The system of public works of a country, state, or region.
Interest rate	The proportion of a loan that is charged as interest to the borrower, typically expressed as an annual percentage of the loan outstanding.
Islam	The religious faith of Muslims including belief in Allah as the sole deity and in Muhammad as his prophet.
Land reclamation	The process of creating new land from oceans, riverbeds, or lake beds.
Landmass	A large area of land.
Malay	A member of a people of the Malay Peninsula, eastern Sumatra, parts of Borneo, and some adjacent islands.
Mandarin	The chief dialect of China.
Maritime	Of or relating to ocean navigation or trade.
Mongol	A member of any of a group of traditionally pastoral peoples of Mongolia.
Monsoon	The rainy season that occurs in southern Asia in the summer.
Mortality rate	The number of a particular group who die each year.
Natural resource	Something (as water, a mineral, forest, or kind of animal) that is found in nature and is valuable to humans.
Peninsula	A piece of land extending out into a body of water.
Precipitation	Water that falls to the earth as hail, mist, rain, sleet, or snow.
Recession	A period of reduced business activity.
Republic	A country with elected representatives and an elected chief of state who is not a monarch and who is usually a president.
Ring of Fire	Belt of volcanoes and frequent seismic activity nearly encircling the Pacific Ocean.
Shintoism	The indigenous religion of Japan.
Street food	Prepared or cooked food sold by vendors in a street or other public location for immediate consumption.
Sultan	A ruler especially of a Muslim state.
Taoism	A religion developed from Taoist philosophy and folk and Buddhist religion and concerned with obtaining long life and good fortune often by magical means.
Tiger economy	A tiger economy is a nickname given to several booming economies in Southeast Asia.
Typhoon	A hurricane occurring especially in the region of the Philippines or the China Sea.
Urbanization	The process by which towns and cities are formed and become larger as more and more people begin living and working in central areas.

Chronology

c. 3000 BCE:	The Phung Nguyen culture.
1–100 CE:	Buddhism appears in Chiao Chih, coming from the countries of China and India.
939:	A Chinese force is defeated by Ngo Quyen, which ends political domination by the Chinese.
1428–1527:	During the Second Golden Age of the Le Dynasty in Dai Viet, the Nguyen Trai and Le Loi lead a revolt against the Ming, with an independent dynasty established; the attack of Champa occurs; and Le Thanh Tong implements the changes as king.
1771–1802:	The Tay Son Rebellion, when the Tay Son brothers defeat the Trinh and Nguyen and work to unify the country.
1802–1945:	Period of French control of Vietnam, which is divided into three parts: Tonkin, Annam, and Cochinchina.
1859–1945:	Period of French control of Vietnam, which is divided into three parts: Tonkin, Annam, and Cochinchina.
1956–1975:	The Vietnam War, aka the American War.
1968:	The Tet Offensive takes place.
1975:	The United States and all foreign support leave Vietnam.
1976:	Saigon is renamed Ho Chi Minh City. Socialist Republic of Vietnam proclaimed. Hundreds of thousands of refugees "boat people" flee from the country.
1979:	Vietnam invades Cambodia.
1986:	Nguyen Van Linh becomes party leader and introduces a more flexible economic policy.
2008:	Vietnam launches first communications satellite from French Guiana.
2011:	China and Vietnam sign an agreement to manage the South China Sea dispute. It includes a hotline to deal with emergencies and a provision for twice-yearly bilateral meetings.
2016:	US lifts long-standing ban on selling weapons to Vietnam.
2017	Vietnam introduces draft law requiring all adult citizens to donate blood once a month due to a shortage at national blood banks.

Further Reading

nh, Pham Tran. *History of Vietnam: The Origin of the Vietnamese People*. USA: Basic Books, 2017.

Churchman, Catherine. *The People Between the Rivers: The Rise and Fall of the Bronze Drum Culture*. Maryland: Rowman & Littlefield, 2016.

Diamond, Chris. *The Secrets of Ho Chi Minh*. USA: Chris Diamond, 2016.

Drollette, Dan Jr. *Gold Rush in the Jungle: The Race to Discover & Defend the Rarest Animals of Vietnam's "Lost World."* New York: Crown Publishing, 2013.

ahdi, Thomas. *Vietnam in the Global Economy: The Dynamics of Integration, Decentralization, and Contested Politics*. Maryland: Lexington Books, 2013.

Internet Resources

ttps://www.worldatlas.com/webimage/countrys/asia/vietnam/vnland.htm
he World Atlas supplies geographical information on Vietnam, as well as fast facts, eather, travel info, and more.

ttps://www.pbs.org/hanoi/vietnam.htm
BS offers many articles on Vietnam and its history.

ietnam. https://www.cfr.org/backgrounder/surging-vietnamese-economy
he Council on Foreign Relations provides articles on the world economy that clude Vietnam.

ietnamese culture. http://vietnamembassy-usa.org/vietnam/culture
he website of the Embassy of the Socialist Republic of Vietnam provides cultural formation on family life, local dress, major festivals, literature, and many other eas of Vietnamese culture.

Index